Patients as Partners

The Trust-Based Approach to **Grow** Your **Medical Practice**

Patients as Partners

The Trust-Based Approach to **Grow** Your **Medical Practice**

DR. VINAY GARODIA

Available on amazonkindle

Worldwide Published by

Pendown Press

PREMIUM BUSINESS PUBLISHER

PENDOWN PRESS LLP

An ISO 9001 & ISO 14001 Certified Co.,

Regd. Office: 3767A, Kanhaiya Nagar,

Tri Nagar, Delhi-110035

Ph.: 8130886000, 9650072927

E-mail: info@pendownpress.com

Branch Office: 1A/2A, 20, Hari Sadan, Ansari Road,

Daryaganj, New Delhi-110002

Ph.: 011-45794768

Website: PendownPress.com

Edition: 2025

Price: ₹ 399

ISBN: 978-93-6338-073-8

Layout and Cover Designed by Pendown Graphics Team

Printed and Bound in India by Thomson Press India Ltd.

TABLE OF CONTENTS

A FOREWORD ABOUT THE AUTHOR

I have had the pleasure of knowing Dr. Vinay Garodia for over three decades. Vinay joined the MBBS course at AIIMS a year after I did. Since then, Vinay has been a friend, colleague, and fellow traveler in the ever-evolving journey in the field of medicine. From our early days at AIIMS learning the nuances of clinical medicine to the distinguished career he has had, one thing has remained constant: Vinay's unwavering integrity and deep commitment to his patients.

Vinay is a nationally respected Eye and Retina Specialist, known for his clinical acumen, surgical expertise, and a calm, thoughtful approach to patient care. A gold medalist in MD Ophthalmology from AIIMS, he is also a DNB, MNAMS, and FRCS (Edinburgh); but beyond his credentials, it is his clarity of purpose and sincerity of practice that stand out.

As the Founder Director of a leading eye care center in Delhi NCR, he has created a space where ethics, excellence, and empathy thrive. The practice is one of the region's most trusted names in ophthalmology, with over 25 senior visiting specialists. Many choose to work with him for the collaborative and respectful environment he has fostered.

Vinay has mentored many young ophthalmologists, assisting them in improving their clinical and surgical skills, as well as their communication, trust-building, and humane practices. His mentees often refer to him with respect and appreciation.

What many may not know- but those of us who've known him well truly value- is his sharp, witty sense of humor, which he has retained through all of life's ups and downs. It's that same dry wit that makes his company enjoyable and his perspective refreshingly honest. Vinay believes in telling things as they are- no frills, no pretence - and that honesty, paired with compassion, is what makes him such a trusted figure in both professional and personal circles.

His patients frequently report experiencing a sense of being heard, understood, and secure under his care, which is considered one of the highest accolades a doctor can attain in our profession. Especially in the management of complex retinal cases and of surgical complications, his balanced judgment, ethical clarity, and patient-first attitude have earned him the trust of both patients and peers.

This book is not a theoretical treatise. It reflects the experience of building a successful medical practice through values, not numbers. It is Vinay's way of sharing what truly matters in medicine- and I believe it will serve as a meaningful guide for every Doctor seeking to grow with grace and stay rooted in purpose.

Dr. Rakesh Lodha

Professor, Department of Pediatrics, and Associate Dean (Academics), All India Institute of Medical Sciences (AIIMS), New Delhi

PREFACE

In today's rapidly evolving world of medicine, clinical excellence alone is no longer enough. While knowledge and surgical skill form the foundation of good practice, the true measure of a successful healthcare journey lies in how we communicate, support, and serve — not just as doctors, but as fellow human beings.

What matters most is not just what we do for patients but how we make them feel. A diagnosis delivered with empathy, a complication handled with honesty, a moment of silence offered during their anxiety — these are lessons no textbook can teach. Yet, these moments, repeated with sincerity, build a kind of trust that no marketing campaign can buy.

This book is my humble attempt to share insights gained over nearly three decades as an ophthalmologist, surgeon, mentor, and lifelong student of human behaviour.

During my medical training at AIIMS, I received what I consider the finest clinical and surgical education possible. Yet, as I stepped into independent practice, I realised how much more there was to learn — about people, emotions, fear and reassurance, and above all, about trust. No one prepares you for the deep human complexity of being a doctor in real life.

Patients as Partners: The Trust-Based Approach to Grow Your Medical Practice is born from this understanding. It offers a counter-narrative to the growing pressure on doctors to "market" themselves, chase visibility, and sacrifice values for volume. There is a better way — one built on respect, transparency, and genuine partnership.

Over the years, I have built a high-trust, high-impact practice that has grown steadily, ethically, and organically. I have worked with patients from diverse backgrounds, managed both straightforward cases and complex complications, and witnessed firsthand the power of honesty in difficult conversations. When patients feel truly seen and heard, trust flourishes.

This book does not offer quick formulas or textbook theories. Instead, it shares stories — personal, practical, and proven — of learning, humility, and healing. Stories of patients who taught me as much as I helped them, and of how trust can transform even the most challenging situations into meaningful connections.

You will also find insights medical school never provided: how to build a reputation without self-promotion, face complications without fear, and run a practice that brings peace of mind, not just a busy schedule.

This book is for young doctors beginning their journey and wondering how to grow with grace and integrity. It is also for seasoned professionals who feel the fatigue of transactional care and are searching for something deeper, more human.

You don't need to chase patients. When you practice with sincerity, empathy, and integrity, they will find their way to you. When you treat them as partners, they stay, not just for treatment, but for a lifetime.

If this book helps you rediscover the joy of being a doctor, build trust, create impact, and lead with compassion, then my purpose in writing it will be fulfilled.

With warmth and solidarity,

Dr. Vinay Garodia

MBBS (AIIMS), MD (AIIMS, Gold Medalist), DNB, MNAMS, FRCS (Ed)

Founder Director, Synergy Eye Care, Delhi NCR

Chapter 1

Patients will Chase Us, ONLY If We Don't Chase Them The Power of Non-Pushy Practice

An Invaluable Lesson Learned The Hard Way!

This occurred during the early stages of my private practice, less than a year after I left AIIMS. I saw a patient who had been blind in one eye for a long time and came to me with a sudden loss of vision in his only seeing eye.

After examining the patient, **I discovered that he had a recent retinal detachment in his only seeing eye. This condition is sight-threatening and requires urgent surgery to save and restore vision.**

I was highly concerned since this was the patient's only functional eye, and I advised him to undergo retinal surgery as soon as possible. I explained that delaying the surgery could significantly reduce the chances of a successful outcome and hinder his recovery of vision.

Driven by my commitment to do the best for my

patient and to ensure he did not lose vision in his only seeing eye, I offered to perform the surgery either the same day or the following day. I even proposed that if he was not ready with the finances, I would proceed with the surgery anyway, allowing him to pay later. I emphasised that the surgery should not be delayed due to financial constraints.

Unfortunately, despite my intentions to help, the patient perceived my eagerness to operate in a different way. He became frightened and lost trust in me, ultimately deciding against the surgery. He left my clinic with his attendant, stating that he would think about it later.

Even after 23 years, I still remember that scene when the patient who could not see left with his attendant, and I could do nothing but watch helplessly. **I was so concerned for him that I am sure if I were allowed to do a forceful surgery, I would have done it. Sadly, I couldn't do anything.**

Later, in hindsight, I realised I had not followed the correct sequence of approaching the whole situation, which I will be sharing below. **I was seen as too eager to operate, and I was seen as someone chasing this patient, and it scared him away.**

In my current stage of practice, this is how I proceed—

- I educate the patient and inform them about the need for surgery and its urgency.
- After this, I would tell them they should think about it and get operated on as soon as possible, wherever they feel more comfortable.

- What I have realised is that now that I am not seen as running after them, they become more keen to get operated on by me and invariably book their surgery then and there.
- And they also feel good about having had a chance to decide for themselves rather than being pressured into it.

What I have realised in my almost three decades of experience of dealing with patients is that if we chase after patients, we scare them away. Instead, when we educate the patient and tell them that we are available for them, they chase us and come to us.

Marketing is the art of making the customer/patient want to buy/take services from us.

People don't like to be sold to; they want to buy.

Present ourselves, our centre, and our services in such a way to our patients that they become eager to take the services (procedures/surgery) from us. If we directly advise the patient about surgery, they may become defensive or suspicious and decide not to proceed with us.

A proper sequence has to be followed in every interaction with the patient. First of all, when the patient meets us, they should in their minds know and believe that they are meeting an 'Expert'.

Establishing our authority as an expert should begin from the moment the patient becomes aware of us. Patients can have experiences at various points in their journey. This can occur during the appointment booking process, while browsing our website or online appointment page, upon arrival at our centre or clinic, when interacting with the receptionist, while waiting in the waiting area, during the examination with our assistant or optometrist, and when entering the examination room, among other instances.

After we have examined the patient, don't be in a rush to suggest the required surgery. Before this, give them something valuable that makes them begin to trust us and our capabilities more. This can include education about their disease and debunking some myths they may have about their health or disease.

After this, summarise the situation for them and then give them the options.

- One option is to do nothing, which could result in either the problem continuing or even risking vision loss, depending on the case.
- The other option, of course, will be the surgery or treatment plan we recommend for their situation.

At this time, the patient should not feel pressured into making a decision to undergo surgery. Instead, they should feel like they are talking to an expert who is there to help them. This conversation should be conducted in a friendly manner to establish that we intend to help them navigate the situation rather than 'sell' our surgery. Give them enough time and answer all their questions. It is made easier at this stage because we have already educated the patient. Therefore, the patient has more realistic expectations. Additionally, previous education enables them to understand the risks of the surgery better, and they can be gently informed that there are no guarantees of results, only promises of effort (more on this in a later chapter).

Building Trust & Expertise Through Education & Transparency

Many times, we get patients who ask if they have a cataract or who have been told that they have a cataract, and they need to be operated on at the earliest. In these situations, I tell them that I don't care if they have a cataract or not, as surgery is not required if the patient is not inconvenienced by the decrease in vision caused by the cataract.

Hearing this is a novelty for a patient who has been told everywhere that they need to undergo surgery quickly. Then I go on to explain that cataract surgery is not an urgent procedure, as we regain lost vision after the operation, so there is no need to rush into surgery.

I also explain to them that we don't have to wait for the cataract to fully mature (or ripen) before operating, and we will operate whenever the patient is having inconvenience. If they can carry on their daily activities comfortably without any challenge, then there is no need to operate right now. If individuals encounter difficulties in their daily work, they should not suffer unnecessarily. They should consider undergoing a short, painless cataract surgery that has excellent results in most cases and involves minimal morbidity. This helps build trust and serves as a guarantee that whenever this patient experiences visual problems due to cataracts, they will always return to us for treatment.

Similarly, whenever a young patient comes in to inquire

about LASIK laser or other refractive surgery to remove glasses. The first thing I tell them is that it is an optional surgery, not an essential one. This is required only for cosmetic or convenience purposes.

After this, once the patient is keen on surgery, we examine them and explain the options. By doing this, we establish that we are not merely running after the surgery; instead, we emerge as experts who help patients make informed decisions. This ensures that the patient has more trust in us and also that they do not have any unrealistic expectations from the surgery.

In contrast, if we push the patient to undergo surgery, they will expect super-normal vision and have unrealistic expectations from the surgery and, hence, are more likely to be disappointed with the results.

Key Takeaways

1. Give value to our patients and give them time to absorb our suggestions.
2. Don't push them for treatment or surgery.
3. Don't show our eagerness or desperation to the patient (even though it is out of concern); educate them instead.
4. Establish trust and expertise to make the patient eager to use our services.
5. The discussion about the surgery, procedures, and finances involved should be more conversational rather than transactional.

Chapter 2

Don't be the "Jack of All, Master of None". Be a Specialist, Not a Generalist Our 'Limited Competence' Can Win Trust

Transparency is The Key to Trust

Once, I had a patient who came to me from Meerut because he had heard good reviews about me and was referred by a patient of mine. **This patient had a corneal ulcer, which was being treated by a local ophthalmologist at Meerut, who was a cornea specialist.**

When I saw the patient, **I informed him that he was being treated properly by a competent cornea specialist and that the treatment being offered was the correct one.** I went on to **tell him that his treating Doctor was probably more qualified than I and more suitable for handling this serious corneal condition** for two reasons:

One, because he was a cornea specialist and knew more about cornea than I did.

Secondly, because this condition requires regular follow-ups and close monitoring, it would be better if he were treated by a local doctor rather than an out-of-town doctor.

After this, contrary to what many people might believe, the patient did not think of me as an incompetent doctor (for having said that his treating Doctor was more qualified than I was).

He instead thought of me as an honest doctor, and he understood that I am an expert specialist in my field of retina, cataract, and refractive surgery.

He went back to his treating ophthalmologist and narrated the story to him. I received a call from this ophthalmologist, and he thanked me and became a fan, referring many retinal patients to me.

This simple act of offering an honest opinion, which kept the patient's interest in mind, resulted in a slight loss of consultation fee, **but it helped me gain fans (both patients and ophthalmologists) and ultimately led to an increase in patients and revenue.**

If we want to establish our credentials as an Expert in some field, we also have to show that there are certain fields where we are not an expert.

We cannot be the 'Jack of All and Master of None'.

However, it is difficult to tell a patient who comes to us that we are not an expert in the disease that he is suffering from. We fear that the patient will judge us and think that we are not qualified enough. Someone, especially in the initial stages of practice, may operate from the level of desperation. It is tempting to treat the patient, even with our sub-optimal level of expertise, or to call someone to do the procedure without the patient knowing that we are not the ones doing the surgery. The disadvantage of this approach is that the suboptimal results the patient receives would tarnish our reputation, especially in the initial stages of our career. Even more importantly, we would not feel comfortable with it, and this lack of confidence would be evident on our faces when interacting with patients. These patients would likely never be satisfied with us and would likely never refer any more patients to us, which could damage our reputation and that of our practice.

I am a Retina Specialist who also performs cataract and Refractive surgeries. I tell my patients very clearly that I do only these surgeries. I refer all other speciality cases, such as Cornea, Oculoplasty, Glaucoma, Squint, etc., to the specialists on my team.

There are multiple advantages to following this philosophy.

1. We give the best possible treatment to the patient
2. We need not lie to the patient. Remember, the so-called Shadow Surgery is not only ethically wrong, but it is also

tough to hide who is actually performing the surgery. Once the patient discovers that they were lied to, we will never be able to regain their trust, let alone win their loyalty.

3. If we do not transfer the responsibility for managing this patient to the expert surgeon, there are two likely problems. The expert Doctor may not be able to treat the patient to the best of his abilities because of our interference. Additionally, we and the expert doctors may end up giving the patient two different pieces of information, which could lead to a loss of credibility and trust.
4. It saves our time not being in the OT, pretending we are operating, and we can let the expert surgeon (in that field) operate while we are doing some other more productive work.
5. When we inform the patient that we want their eye to receive the best possible treatment, even if it means not operating ourselves and sharing the revenues with another expert surgeon, the patient develops more trust in us and is more likely to return to us and refer patients.
6. When we inform the patient that we will not be performing a particular type of surgery, as we are not the best in this sub-speciality, the patient also understands and believes that we are the best in whatever we do. We establish ourselves as the domain experts in our field (Retina, Cataract, and Refractive surgeries in my case). He is more likely to come to us for these problems and refer patients to us in the future.

So, in a nutshell, if we want to establish ourselves as experts in our specialised fields, we have to make it clear to the patient that there are other better persons (in our team or circle) who will deal with situations where we are not experts. This would help us establish our **authority** and also build **trust**. Both these factors are essential in getting more referrals from our patients.

Key Takeaways

1. Be an Expert in what we do and give it our best.
2. Be confident and honest in telling patients about our limitations.
3. Refer the patient to the best possible Expert in the field.
4. This will build our Trust and Credibility and will be highly beneficial and profitable for us in the long run.

Chapter 3

Be Human, NOT GOD: Never Promise, Always Deliver Manage Expectations with Humility

A Doctor is Human, Not GOD!

A young 25-year-old diabetic girl came to me with loss of vision in both eyes due to severe Proliferative Diabetic Retinopathy with Vitreous Haemorrhage and Tractional Retinal Detachment in both eyes.

Of course, the patient and her parents were quite worried about the situation. They consulted a few ophthalmologists and were aware of the seriousness of the situation. One of them then suggested me for the treatment. They came to me with a lot of hope, and her father told me,

"Doctor, please save her. We have come to you with lots of hope, and you are God for us".

As is my habit, **I immediately corrected him and told him that I would do whatever best I could, but I am no God or even close to Him.**

We are all humans dealing with human bodies, so one can never be sure of the results. **I cannot guarantee the results, but I can guarantee our efforts,** and God willing, she should improve her vision.

We evaluated her eyes with ultrasonography and found the left eye to be worse compared to the other. We operated on the right eye with a better prognosis first, and even this surgery turned out to be a very challenging one. After the surgery, we informed the parents about the seriousness of the situation and gave a guarded prognosis for the surgery's results.

As luck would have it, this patient recovered with an excellent vision of 6/12 in her right eye postoperatively. The patient, her family, and I were delighted with the results.

The patient and the parents were very thankful to me. I told them, **"I did my best, but the results are because your eyes responded well to my treatment".** I further told them, "Every good result also makes me happy, so I must thank you and your eyes and your luck that we have got good results, and I thank you for making my day better because of this excellent result".

A week after this, we took up surgery for her left eye, which had a worse prognosis.

As expected, the retinal condition was extremely bad. After surgery, the patient did not get as good a vision in this eye. **She could recover only 6/60 vision in this eye and then had a rebleed in this eye, leading to further loss of vision.**

In a typical scenario, the patient and the family would have been very disappointed. **However, because the family had seen me not taking credit for the good results, they also understood that the bad results were not within my control. They continued to have faith in me and allowed me to operate once again on her left eye.**

This time, after a very challenging surgery, we could remove some remaining traction from her retina. **After 4-6 weeks of this second surgery, the left eye could also gain some functional vision of 6/24.**

Never feel that we are God. Have humility always. If a patient calls us God, we should immediately be very wary. The patient who calls us God would often expect Miracles from us and will likely be dissatisfied with the less-than-miraculous results. Therefore, it is better to cap the patient's expectations and remain humble in the face of all the praise.

On a lighter note, one must remember that whenever things don't go the way we want, God is often the first one to be blamed. **So, it is better for our sanity and peace of mind to avoid this God complex.**

The most common mistake doctors make is that they take credit for the good results of their surgeries and refuse to take responsibility for the bad results, instead blaming them on bad luck or other factors.

What I consistently follow is that when we achieve good results (which is far more common than when we have bad results), I don't take credit when the patient praises me. My saying this doesn't take away any credit from me in the patient's mind. Instead, they realise that I am a humble and grounded person and appreciate me even more for this. I also acknowledge that this is not a one man's job, and we (the patient and I) are in it together (more on the concept of Synergy: Partner in Eye Care later). We both share responsibility for the good or bad results.

Once we do this consistently with each and every patient, this message gets conveyed to our staff and other patients as well, and it becomes the culture of the practice.

Approaching a situation like this makes it much easier to handhold the patient in cases where we don't get the desired results, or we face any complications, because the patient realises that it is not my mistake but depends on many more factors.

Do not take the blame for the sub-optimal or poor results. However, do not shy away from responsibility **(which is not the same as blame)** and provide a lot of support to manage the complications or to help them understand the situation and assist in whatever manner possible.

We must be present for the patient without any guilt, with genuine concern, and with the intention to help. This helps us convert even patients who have had sub-optimal results. They, too, trust us and are impressed with our sincerity and handholding, and become our fans (more about this in another chapter).

Never Promise, Always Deliver

Once we make it a point to educate the patients and involve them in decision-making, this question of promise is generally taken care of.

**We must promise our efforts,
but never promise the results.**

Remember the teaching from the Gita,

"Karm karo, Phal Ki Chinta Mat Karo"
(Do your duty, and don't be fixated on the results.)

It is acceptable to prognosticate and inform the patient of the chances of success in general terms while reassuring them. Still, it is not advisable to promise any result to the patient. We can promise to put in the effort and over-deliver by being there with patients if things are not going as expected.

The key is to draw the patient's attention to our efforts rather than fixating solely on the results.

This dictum of not promising results has to be followed by everyone in the organisation. This way, even our staff and colleagues can confidently inform patients and their families that we don't promise specific results.

This is especially needed when we are dealing with complicated surgeries like those for Retina, Glaucoma, Cornea, etc. It is also applicable for routine surgeries with good prognoses, such as cataracts and LASIK, as well, since the results are not always as expected.

Whenever in doubt about the prognosis, always give a guarded prognosis. For example, if we are operating on a cataract and find mild degeneration in the macula, it is better to give a guarded prognosis. Postoperatively, if we get good results, we can always celebrate this with the patient. I often jokingly tell them,

"You have proven me wrong by getting better results than what I had predicted, and I am so happy to be proven wrong".

This kind of friendly talk shows that we are happy with the patient's well-being, we are humble, and the patients also remember this good feeling, which makes them become our fans.

Key Takeaways

1. Don't feel like God, and definitely resist being labelled as God.
2. Be a humble and confident Human.
3. Do not take Solo Credit for your Good results. Take Responsibility (and not Blame) for the bad results, and be with the patient to handhold them even in the case of disappointing results.
4. Never promise results; promise your efforts, even in a simple, good prognosis case.
5. Everyone in our organisation should follow these principles universally.

Chapter 4

Had a Complication? Take the Credit, Not the Blame. RUN ...... Towards (Not Away From) The Patient

An Eventful Conference: Learning At Its Best!

While attending a Live Surgery Session as an operating surgeon at a conference, I was observing other expert surgeons performing flawless surgeries with no complications. **And then, one of my colleagues had a complication during the surgery** in front of the whole audience.

The surgeon was an accomplished professional, and he managed the complication in a methodical, scientific, and skilful manner, ultimately completing the case successfully.

If I were a judge for the event and had to award the best surgery medal to a person, I would have given it not to the people who performed flawless surgeries but to the surgeon who had a complication and still managed it confidently and correctly in front of everyone.

I personally went to him and congratulated him.

- A great surgeon is not the one who can do good, uneventful surgery.
- A great surgeon is one who manages complications with composure and finesse to produce good results.
- An exceptional surgeon is one who has just managed a complication and then continues with the rest of the surgeries without any apprehension.

Are there any surgeons who will never have any complications?

There can be only two such possibilities:

- Those who don't operate
- And those who lie

Complications in a surgery, or for that matter, any procedure, are very much part of the game. The results of surgery in most routine cases have become very predictable nowadays, especially in the hands of skilled surgeons. When we consistently deliver excellent results, we often start to expect and believe that we will never face any complications.

Often, we make the mistake of starting to believe ourselves to be 'God'. So whenever we do, unfortunately, have a complication, we tend to get into denial mode. We feel scared that the patient will reject any complication and will think we are incompetent, negligent, or unethical due to this. We forget that we are humans operating on human eyes, and sometimes complications will occur.

The biggest mistake surgeons make is either trying to hide the complication by not informing the patient and fudging the medical records, or by feeling guilty for having the complication.

Hiding the complication or fudging the records is a big No-No, not only ethically but also legally.

Doing this can land us in a big legal mess. The law recognises it to be okay to have a complication as long as we are practising with a standard of care expected of us. However, the law is stringent against hiding complications or falsifying records. One must NEVER do this.

Moreover, when we intend to conceal the complication, we may inadvertently perform certain surgical steps that can be harmful to the patient.

For example, in a cataract surgery with a posterior capsular (PC) rent, we may not perform the required anterior vitrectomy or may not change the intraocular lens (IOL) to be implanted, which could conceal the complication from the patient, potentially with serious ramifications for the patient's eye and vision.

The other mistake, being too defensive and guilty about having a complication, is also not advisable. We have to realise that we had a complication, which is unfortunate but an integral part of surgical practice.

If we are too defensive and behave like a guilty person, there can be multiple disadvantages:

- We will lose the trust of the patient, and they will consider us a bad surgeon, never coming back to us.
- The patient is more likely to file a medico-legal case against us.
- Most importantly, if the patient loses trust in us, they are likely to stop taking proper treatment for their disease and may search for another doctor to manage the complication. Thus, they may not receive the best possible treatment because this other Doctor may not be as competent as we are in managing this complication. Moreover, this other Doctor would not be precisely aware of what happened during the surgery, and hence, even if competent, cannot provide the best possible treatment.

So, what I do is as follows:

In patients where we expect a higher risk of complications, such as in the case of posterior polar cataract, I forewarn the patient about this and reassure them that we will take extra precautions in this case and have a backup option to manage potential complications, like vitrectomy, ready as well. The advantage of explaining the procedure to the patient beforehand is that, if we don't encounter any complications, they appreciate our expertise in managing the situation effectively. If we had not explained the possible complications, the patients and their attendants would not have appreciated the extra surgical expertise that we invested in managing this complex surgery.

If a complication does occur, we are better prepared to handle it, and there is no psychological pressure on us in the operating theatre, as the patient has already been informed. After the surgery, the patient and attendants are immediately told about the complication and reassured that, since we were prepared, we managed it well. The patient is further informed that, due to the complicated surgery, they should not expect a recovery as fast as in a typical case, so their expectations are limited.

I have an interesting anecdote on this, too.

Keeping Communication Crystal Clear

My MBBS batchmate once asked me to operate on his mother for cataract. I called Auntie for the surgery: I had never examined her before this. **When she came for the surgery, I examined her eyes and found that the cataract was posterior polar.**

Before taking her up for surgery, **I informed my friend of the higher risk of nucleus drop and the possible need for a vitrectomy.**

Then, when I went in for surgery, lo and behold, I did have a nucleus drop. Since I was prepared, we immediately did vitrectomy and phacofragmentation and implanted a 3-piece IOL in that surgery.

After the surgery, it was much easier for me to explain the complication to my friend, and he was also satisfied with the management. Auntie gained a complete 6/6 vision.

If I had not forewarned my friend about this higher risk of complications before surgery, I would have found it very difficult to explain this situation after surgery.

Whatever reason I would have given after surgery would have sounded like an excuse, and he would have felt that I was trying to cover up my mistake.

In case of unexpected complication during surgery, where the patient has not been fore-warned about the increased risk of complication, we do manage the complication in the best possible manner (we have the emergency backup protocols ready for these complications in our OT and the staff is well trained to immediately recognise the complication and arrange the machines, IOls etc. for vitrectomy or other procedures).

- Immediately after the surgery, the patient and the attendants are informed about the complications. **It is best to report the complication on the same day, immediately after it occurs.** The immediate post-operative period is the time when the patient and attendants are most anxious and are more likely to accept the fact that a complication has occurred. If we conceal the complication at this time and inform them about it a few days later (or worse, if they discover it from another doctor), then the patient will never be able to trust us.
- We must remain non-defensive when speaking with patients or their attendants. **We should not take the blame for the complication, but instead, take credit for managing it well.** We should explain to them that despite the complication that occurred, we managed it in the best possible manner in a very efficient way because our systems are always well-prepared.
- Even in cases where more than standard manipulation is required and **we expect more inflammation after surgery, it is better to forewarn the patient that the post-op vision recovery may not be as rapid and may be delayed.** If the post-op recovery is slow, the patient feels better that they

were forewarned. In case they do better than expected, then I tell them jokingly, "You proved me wrong. I was expecting a slower recovery, but your body responded much better than I expected." This statement relieves the anxiety they had, and a friendly bond is formed.

Had a Complication? RUN ..... Towards (Not Away From) the Patient

It is a common, though unfortunate, practice that when a surgeon faces a complication, they become apprehensive about meeting the patient and their attendants because they feel uncomfortable seeing their 'failure' and don't like the awkward questions that are posed to them. This may lead to them avoiding the patient and attendants during the post-operative period by either not being available to them or assigning this 'unpleasant' task to another associate doctor on their team.

This practice of running away from the patient is wrong for the following ethical and practical reasons:

- **The patient's medical care suffers because the surgeon is the best person** to manage this difficult post-operative situation. By not being available to the patient, the medical management is likely to be compromised, resulting in even worse outcomes.
- **The patient and attendants feel dissatisfied and cheated**, as they believe they are not being adequately cared for and are not receiving the best possible care. They are forced to seek another opinion from another doctor, who may not be very charitable towards the surgeon, and may increase the distrust between the patient and the surgeon even more.

- **A dissatisfied patient and attendant are more likely to spread negative words and reviews** about the surgeon. **They are also more likely to pursue legal recourse,** which increases the difficulties for the surgeon. If the case goes to court, the fact that the surgeon did not adequately care for the patient after the complication will be used against the surgeon.

There is no crime in having a complication. Still, it is criminal and ethically wrong not to manage the complication properly.

So, when we encounter a complication, we must go out of our way to interact with the patient and attendants, giving them all the attention and extra time to answer their questions.

In a regular patient, we can get away with fewer interactions and delegate this job to our Assistant Doctors. Still, **in the case of a complication, the primary operating surgeon must take charge of the situation.**

Be there for the patient and attendants for the post-operative period. Tell them how to reach us whenever they have a question or a concern to report. If the patient requires any additional procedure due to a surgical complication, perform it ourself or arrange for it with a relevant expert who specialises in managing such complications.

Keep track of the patient's progress, not to escape liabilities, but out of genuine concern for the patient. The patient and attendants can easily sense and judge whether we are enquiring about them from genuine concern or just fear of litigation. Throughout this process, we must remember not to become too defensive or guilty in our approach. Be firm with genuine concern and empathy.

Don't Let a Complication Go to Waste: Make the Patient Your Fan for Life

Complications, though inevitable, are fortunately a very uncommon occurrence in a surgeon's life.

We have to leave no stone unturned to manage it well to the best of our abilities. If we or our setup is not the best equipped to handle the complication, we must refer them to a more suited person or centre. We must not restrict the best possible treatment due to cost factors or effort factors. The extra effort or financial resources required for managing these infrequent complications are definitely worth it. They will save us from future guilt and medical and legal consequences.

Having said that, since the complications are a very uncommon occurrence, we must also not lose this 'opportunity in crisis.'

We have all learnt from doing successful surgeries, but we have learnt the most from our own or others' complications. So, if we have a complication, our priority is to help the patient, but also think about how we can 'benefit' from it as well.

Here are a few points where we can 'benefit' from these complications:

1. We need to analyse and learn from what went wrong, identifying lessons that can be learned from the experience. This will involve conducting a Root Cause Analysis (RCA)

and implementing a Corrective Action and Preventive Action (CAPA) plan.

2. We must have a protocol in place in the Operation Theatres (OT) to manage these complications promptly and without confusion. We may even conduct mock drills to assess the preparedness of the OT and staff. Everyone in the OT should be aware of what to do in different situations and where to find the necessary machines and instruments for emergency procedures, such as Posterior Capsular Rent and Nucleus Drop.

3. Once we have managed the complication well, we must also pat ourselves and our team on the back for doing a great job managing the complicated situation. We should reanalyse our performance and identify areas for improvement.

4. Every Surgeon and OT should have a tie-up with other doctors, surgeons, and medical centres to accept their patients in case of complications. The understanding may be with Retinal surgeons (to manage complications such as dropped lenses and endophthalmitis), Glaucoma specialists, Cornea specialists, and others. There should be a clear understanding and protocol regarding what the Retinal surgeon expects the Cataract surgeon to do if a complication arises before referring the patient. There must be an understanding that the surgeon to whom the patient is referred does not unnecessarily badmouth the original surgeon, is considerate of the patient's financial concerns, keeps the original surgeon informed while managing the patient, and so on.

5. When we have an uncomplicated surgery, the surgeon typically does not interact with the patient or attendants too frequently. However, if we encounter a complication, we

need to interact with them repeatedly. **We should not consider this more frequent interaction as merely a necessity, but also as an opportunity to develop a better relationship with the family.**

6. The patient and family must be informed that we are with them and will do our best to help. **Remember not to fall into the trap of guaranteeing them that everything will be alright (remember, we have to avoid the temptation of playing God!!).** During these regular interactions, take the time to answer their queries and educate them about the procedure.
7. The patient and family will see the efforts we are making and will remember this even if the medical results are not entirely satisfactory.
8. Most of the time, these patients and their families will become our biggest fans and refer us to their relatives because they realise that we take extra care of all our patients.

Remember

We have NOT ARRIVED when we give 6/6 vision to the patient, and they come back to us for their other eye or their family's eyes. We have TRULY ARRIVED when a patient goes blind in our hands (despite our best efforts), and they still come back to us for their other eye or their family's eyes.

Key Takeaways

1. It is normal to have complications when we do surgery.
2. Whenever possible, warn the patient about potential complications before surgery.
3. When we do have a complication, do not get too defensive. Keep the patient and relatives informed.
4. The best time to inform about the complication is immediately after the surgery.
5. Do not take the blame, but take the credit for managing the complication well.
6. Handholding the patient and attendants with genuine concern is crucial in cases where complications arise.
7. It is unfortunate to have a complication, but there is an 'Opportunity in Crisis' here. This is the best time to convert our patient into a fan by sincerely supporting and being there for them in their time of crisis.

Chapter 5

Help/Praise Your Competitors, and See Our Practice Grow Ethical Collaboration Beats Competition

Positive Ethical Conduct Brings Huge Rewards

During the initial years of my practice, a fellow ophthalmologist referred to me a patient who had a complication during cataract (phacoemulsification) surgery in the form of a dropped lens. **When the patient came to me, he was furious and blamed the initial surgeon for having 'spoiled' his eyes. He said he would never go back to that referring surgeon.**

After examining him, **I told him the following:**

"Complications happen with every surgeon, including myself. It is a part of doing surgeries. What is important is that he referred you to the right place at the right time, and he has done the initial management of the complication effectively, avoiding unnecessary intervention that would have made it more complicated.

It is not the fault of the surgeon, but rather, it is to the credit of the surgeon that he has managed it very well and in a sincere manner, has not tried to hide the complication, and has done what is best for you. I will do the surgery, which is a major surgery, but I am trained to do it, and I give good results in the majority of cases."

After I performed a successful surgery, **the patient recovered with good vision. He was actively sent back to the referring surgeon for follow-ups. When he went back to this surgeon, he showered him with praise for having referred him to the 'right place at the right time in the right condition'.**

He happily got his other eye operated on at the same surgeon's place with good results.

This ethical and straightforward conduct on my part saved the referring surgeon from a medico-legal complication and also made him my fan.

This action also established my credibility among fellow ophthalmologists, demonstrating that I do not badmouth colleagues and that I send them back their referred cases.

This surgeon referred all his retinal patients to me for management enthusiastically and recommended me to many of his ophthalmologist colleagues as well.

Helping our colleagues in times of distress is not only an ethical thing to do, but it is also beneficial for all. Criticising our colleagues is a foolish thing to do, and it is not only detrimental to the working atmosphere in our field, but it is also harmful to us.

Patients today are very smart and can easily see through us if we unnecessarily criticise our colleagues.

If we defend our colleagues, who also happen to be our competitors, our credibility rises in the eyes of our patients.

Whenever I receive a patient referred to me for managing a surgical complication, I follow a protocol similar to the one given above. Invariably, I end up with a more assured patient, good results, and a very relieved and happy referring ophthalmologist.

I often see patients who seek cataract surgery after having the procedure on their other eye with a different surgeon. Generally, I find that the previous surgery is quite decent, and I make it a point to praise the last Doctor's skill. Yet, despite my compliments, no patient has ever said, "I'll go back to that surgeon for my other eye's surgery." It's intriguing how appreciation for one's work doesn't affect their choice of surgeon for the second procedure.

Once they have come to us, there is a reason why they want it done by us. My praise of the other surgeon does not deter them; instead, they appreciate my honesty and become more likely to undergo surgery with me.

Criticising colleagues (our competitors) is never a good idea. First of all, it vitiates the atmosphere. What goes around comes around. If we criticise others, others are more likely to criticise us as well. The atmosphere of practice will become more negative and litigious.

Moreover, by criticising others, we fall in the eyes of our patients. They would never like a doctor who criticises colleagues.

If we criticise someone else, the patient immediately starts losing trust in us and our profession in general.

Being a retinal surgeon, I often get patients who have been operated on for cataracts elsewhere and still do not get good vision. Mostly, it occurs despite a successful cataract surgery, but due to a diseased or unhealthy retina or optic nerve.

Typically, when a patient visits me, they have already been seen by the optometrist, who records the patient's vision and basic parameters in the Electronic Medical Record (EMR). So, I already have an idea, even before I see the patient, that this patient has not experienced significant improvement in vision after cataract surgery.

When I see these patients, even before I do a detailed retinal examination and even before the patients have asked me a question, I do a quick examination of the anterior segment and comment, **"The cataract Surgery has been done well, but I wonder why you didn't get good vision. Let me examine your retina to try to find the reason for this poor vision."**

By doing this, even before the patient asks me whether the previous surgeon made any mistakes, I have allayed their apprehensions and reassured them that the previous surgeon did a decent job, and it wasn't their fault.

This simple routine of allaying the patient's apprehensions has saved many medico-legal troubles for the other surgeons. It increases patients' faith in their doctors. The patient also begins to trust me more because they see that I am not criticising my 'competitors'. Many of them will go back to their operating surgeons and repeat what I told them, which helps me build credibility and respect among my colleagues who don't view themselves as my competitors and are likely to refer more of their retinal patients to me.

I also extend similar courtesy to other physicians who refer their patients to me for an opinion. For example, if a diabetic patient is advised by their physician or endocrinologist to undergo regular retinal checks, I always make it a point to praise the referring physician. I tell that patient that your physician has done a great job by educating you and encouraging you to get a retinal checkup at a regular interval for diabetic changes. You must go back to them with my reports and convey my thanks for taking such good care of you.

This makes the patient more relieved, and when they return to the physician, it also generates a lot of goodwill in the physician's mind towards me, motivating them to educate their patients and refer them to us for a retinal checkup. Therefore, being helpful and praising others helps us grow our practice both ethically and pleasantly.

Key Takeaways

1. Always try to praise our colleagues and competitors genuinely.
2. Criticising other doctors is not only unethical, it is detrimental to our growth and practice.

3. Help our colleagues and competitors, and it will ultimately benefit us.
4. Patients are smart and can easily discern whether we are genuinely interested in their well-being or just trying to one-up other ophthalmologists.
5. Intentional or unintentional criticism of a colleague is the most common cause of medico-legal disputes and dissatisfaction in practice.

Chapter 6

Negative Feedback From Patients is Gold Turn Complaints into Growth

From Anger to Appreciation: The Magic of Accepting Feedback

Once, in my OPD, a patient complained to me about the rude behaviour of one of my staff members. **She was, of course, very upset and agitated.** She told me that another patient was seen out of turn, and when she objected, her objections were brushed aside 'rudely' by one of the staff members.

I immediately apologised for the anguish she had to go through without asking any more questions. Then I went on to thank her for bringing this to my notice, as it shows that she was a well-wisher of mine and wanted to see improvement in my facility.

The moment she heard my apology and appreciation, she immediately relaxed and came into the listening and discussion mode. Then I let her speak freely and tell me the whole story. It turned out that an elderly patient in a wheelchair was seen ahead of her, and she was not informed about the reason for this.

As she was telling me this, I could see that she had begun to realise that possibly the elderly gentleman had been given priority because he was more vulnerable.

I listened to her patiently with full attention. After she had finished, I thanked her once again for taking the pains to point out our problems. Then, I explained to her the reason why this elderly patient in a wheelchair was given priority. I told her that it is a part of our **Vulnerable Patients Policy to provide priority to defined vulnerable patients**. I then went on to say to her that our mistake was that we did not inform her about it, and surely, if she had been told, she would have agreed and not felt bad about it.

I told her that, **thanks to her suggestion, we are now going to train our staff and also add to our Vulnerable Patient Policy to inform other patients when we see a vulnerable patient out of turn. I also told her that we would post a notification in the waiting area regarding our policy** so that, in the future, patients won't feel inconvenienced.

Then I went on to gently defend my staff by acknowledging that it was a management mistake, i.e., my own, that the staff was not adequately trained to explain this. I would use this constructive criticism to improve the systems further positively.

By the end of our conversation, this patient was so satisfied and happy that she became one of my biggest fans and continues to follow up with me regularly.

She comes in with a sense of ownership of my place. She is always giving us suggestions to improve further without any hesitation.

There is no bigger well-wisher of ours than the patient who gives us negative feedback. If someone is dissatisfied with the service, it is far easier to ignore the issue and never return or even spread a negative opinion about the setup to friends and family. We must remember that our hospital industry has become similar to the hospitality industry, where client satisfaction is of utmost importance.

Gone are the days when doctors could afford to be rude to the patients and still have patients coming to them because of their eminence alone.

Many of the negative comments, complaints, and constructive criticisms have helped us improve our services, become better, and have contributed to our growth, resulting in happier and satisfied patients.

To come out and express negative feedback, either in person or by writing a review, takes effort and is done by people who would like you to improve. This is especially true for those who give feedback to us in person.

We must always encourage positive as well as negative feedback and suggestions.

Once a patient or their family gives negative feedback, the first thing I do is acknowledge their efforts and their concerns for my well-being. I thank them for their suggestions and criticisms, and I promise to address them. I take action on their suggestions in front of them, or else I note down their suggestions and follow up with them to provide information about the corrective action taken based on their feedback.

If a patient is complaining, it is best to acknowledge the issue first instead of arguing. Do not blame the staff for the mistakes; however, I, as the owner of the centre, take responsibility.

We must utilise the science of ARC (Affinity, Reality, Communication triangle), where we first acknowledge their Reality and refrain from arguing with them. **Once we understand the patient's perspective, we communicate solutions to them. If there is an explanation, we provide it gently without negating their reality.** This constant communication based on the patient's reality leads to an increase in Affinity, and this, in the long run, converts a patient who was unhappy and dissatisfied with us into our biggest fan.

Not only do we learn and improve from the suggestions and constructive criticisms of our patients and families, but we also make these dissatisfied patients happy and convert them into fans who will refer many more patients to us.

Once again, all this must be done with genuine concern and intention, not just as a show-off. A non-genuine effort may work in the short term, but it is ultimately exposed and erodes all the credibility and trust that we have built with the patient and their family.

Key Takeaways

1. Always respect patients who are making an effort to provide us with negative comments, feedback, and constructive criticism.
2. Listen to them and agree with them before starting to give explanations.
3. Acknowledge their help in improving our systems.
4. If possible, implement those suggestions and inform the patient about the corrective steps and improvements that have been undertaken.

Chapter 7

Win the Child, Own the Family for Life
The Pediatric Loyalty Loop

Just Another Day In The OPD: Glasses are Normal!

Visualise this typical scene in my OPD— Parents come in with their child who has just been prescribed glasses. **The mother is very anxious and unhappy that her child needs glasses.** They often complain and blame the child because the child has been using mobile phones or watching TV excessively, which is why they need glasses. **She then proceeds to ask me to tell the child not to use the mobile or screen, as it would be spoiling their eyes.**

At this stage, **I usually find that the child is confused, dejected, and scared. I immediately take the child's side.** First of all, I tell them that it is perfectly okay to have glasses and that needing glasses is not a disease. Smart people use glasses (and I point to my own glasses for effect), and this kid is smart; therefore, they need glasses.

The moment I say that, I see a smile on the child's face and a look of surprise on the parents' faces. Then, I observe the parents and see if they are wearing glasses or not. If they are not wearing glasses, I will joke that the parents are jealous of the child because the child is more intelligent (and needs glasses) compared to the parents. If they are wearing glasses, I would, in a dramatic tone, tell them it is not the child's fault that he has glasses, but rather it is the parents' fault. The child has glasses in his genes.

All this drama puts the child at ease, and they begin to develop some liking and trust in me. The parents, of course, are a bit bewildered because they are hearing something very different from what they are accustomed to believing.

Then, after having won the child's trust**, I proceed to speak directly to the child**. I tell them that they are a smart and grown-up child, so I would be directly talking to them and not to their parents. **The child feels important.** Then I tell them that they will need glasses and which colour frame they would like. I make it a pleasant conversation for the child. Then, somewhere in our discussion, I slip in that, yes, I understand they cannot do without the screen; none of us can, but they should be more mindful of how they use it. I educate them about the importance of blinking regularly, taking frequent breaks, maintaining a comfortable distance, and other related topics. I also encourage them to spend more time outdoors and play physical sports. When I talk directly to the child, they are in a more listening mode, and they understand that I am on their side and am not just repeating their mother's instructions. They also feel more responsible. I often tell them that if they don't follow these simple precautions, it is their eyes that will hurt, not their parents, so it is they who must understand and follow the advice.

At this stage, the parents who were initially shocked by my taking the child's side start to realise that I am, in a subtle manner, educating the child to follow good instructions and develop a liking for me. Now, they also play along.

After this, I will often send the child outside on the pretext of a test, and at this time, I spend 2-5 minutes with the parents to discuss things further. I educate them that we all have a habit of advising them about what to do and what not to do when a child gets glasses. Everyone in the family will be all over the child the moment they find out that they need glasses. They will provide dietary advice, screen usage advice, alternative medicine advice, exercise advice, and more.

The child who was perfectly okay till now will suddenly get bombarded with so much advice that he will get confused that there is something very seriously wrong with them. This kind of feeling can be very detrimental to a child's psyche, and they may develop an inferiority complex.

So, I warn the parents about this and advise them that at least they and their immediate family should accept the glasses as a fact of life and should not let their anxiety be passed on to the child. I reassure them that it is perfectly normal to need glasses and they should not make too much of a fuss about it.

Make it a fun activity for the child and save them from a possible inferiority complex.

I am very fond of children and make friends with them easily. Whenever I get any patient with a child or a child as a patient with their parents, I try to be friendly with the child, as is my nature. I realised during the initial stage of my practice that these families with children developed a liking for me because I was friendly with their children. I could sense an extra affection in this family and child towards me, and that also translated into better patient loyalty. So, I was benefiting from all this, while enjoying what I like to do, i.e., making friends with children.

I have noticed that being friendly with the child earns me the confidence of the parents. They become my biggest fans, never going to any other doctor, and are very comfortable with me. The child also prefers me, and the whole experience becomes enjoyable.

These are a few tips that I found helpful while dealing with children, and I am sharing them here:

- When a child accompanies a patient, do not immediately try to be overly friendly with them. Give them some time to get comfortable in our room. Continue examining the patient and observe the child's curiosity silently. Then, once the examination is over, we can gently say hello to the child or, have a brief conversation or share a joke with them to make them and their parents feel comfortable.
- Consider giving a small item, such as a colouring book with crayons, as a gift to make the child feel welcome and to show the family that we're there.
- When the child is the patient, be gentle with them during the examination.
- Gently acknowledge the discomfort we may have caused them, apologise for it, and also praise them for being so

cooperative during the checkup and treatment.

- Treat the child like an adult and speak directly to them, rather than ignoring the child and only talking to the parents or attendants.
- Explain at least some of our suggestions and precautions directly to the child.
- Give the child a chance to ask questions directly to us.
- If required, take the child's side initially so that they develop more trust in us.

Additionally, consider creating a child-friendly area in our clinic. We can give the children in the waiting room an activity book or a small gift to keep them occupied and happy. Parents love it when their children are given a small gift.

As they say, the way to a man's heart is through his stomach. Similarly, the way to parents' hearts is through their children. Make the child happy, and the parents will be hooked on us.

Key Takeaways

1. Do not ignore children, even when they visit along with a patient.
2. Make the child feel comfortable and welcome.
3. Take the side of the child when they come to us as a patient.
4. Speak directly to the child whenever possible to win their trust and ensure better compliance with our advice.
5. Make the child happy, and the Parents will be ours for life.
6. The love and concern for the child should be genuine and sincere.

Chapter 8

Being Ethical is PROFITABLE
Trust Drives Referrals

The Highest Bungee Jump Serves as a Reaffirmation of My Ethics

I am an adventure sports enthusiast and enjoy activities such as scuba diving, skydiving, paragliding, surfing, and bungee jumping.

The first time I had the opportunity to try bungee jumping was at the Macau Tower when I visited Hong Kong for a conference. I was excited for my first-ever bungee jump and went to the top of the tower for my jump. I was required to sign a significant amount of paperwork to indemnify the company against any potential accidents. **Like everyone else, I signed without reading the details and went up the elevator to reach the platform for the jump.**

The instructor put the safety harness on me. I had no idea what those harnesses and ropes were going to do or whether he was doing his job correctly. I trusted the whole process and believed this guy, who was a total stranger, to do his job well.

When I was at the edge of the platform, at a height of 233 metres (the highest bungee in the world), about to take a jump towards the earth, tied to the harness and ropes for my safety, suddenly a thought came to my mind.

I realised that I was trusting my precious life into the hands of a total stranger, with the belief that he must have done his job thoroughly and accurately, including putting on the safety harnesses, calculating the length of the rope, and ensuring the quality of the rope, among other things. I had to take the 'leap of faith', trusting my life to him and his work ethic.

This moment was a revelation for me about how our patients must feel when they trust us with their precious eyes or bodies. They also sign their consent (mostly without reading it) and allow us to operate on or treat their eyes, trusting that we would be honest and thorough with our work and judgment.

I was filled with a sense of gratitude towards all my past and future patients who have and will trust me with their bodies, lives, and vision. I realised why Trust is so important in our field of work and why we must not ever break this trust.

That day further strengthened my resolve to do my work honestly and to the best of my competence.

During my training at AIIMS, **a common perception existed in academic circles that doctors in private practice are driven by financial gain and often engage in unethical practices.**

The impression was that to survive in practice, one had to do all kinds of unethical or borderline unethical practices, like

- Overprescribing tests
- Hurrying patients for surgery even when they don't need it,
- Pushing them towards more expensive options, even if it is not beneficial for them,
- Engaging in numerous advertising and marketing activities, etc.

When I came out of AIIMS after my training in the so-called 'big bad world of practice', I was scared about how things would work out. The training at AIIMS, or for that matter, at any medical college, doesn't prepare the graduates for the practical world of private practice.

I decided to adhere to ethical practices, knowing it may take longer to start earning. **However, against my expectations, I was able to begin earning well from the start. I realised that there was a lot of value in practising ethically.**

If we work in the best interest of the patient in our mind, the patient realises this and develops trust, coming back to us again and again. Also, they will refer their friends and relatives to us. They would happily pay us an even higher fee compared to other doctors if they see value in us.

Practising ethically is not only more satisfying, much safer, more peaceful, and more enjoyable, but it is also more financially rewarding.

Ethical practice actually helps us earn much more in real life. The myth that money can be made only by unethical means is totally wrong.

Patients in today's world are savvy and can easily spot unethical practices. Sometimes, they may decide to keep quiet because they don't have any other option at the moment. Still, if they are dissatisfied and don't trust us, they will leave us at the first possible opportunity and will never refer any other patient to us.

In today's world of advertising and digital marketing, the cost of acquiring a new patient or lead is high and demanding. Therefore, it would be foolish on our part to make an existing patient dissatisfied, as they may perceive us as being unethical and potentially lose them in the process, resulting in a loss not only to our reputation and peace of mind but also to our finances.

We must strive to make every patient of ours happy with our excellent services and honest approach so that they become our fans, return to us, and refer more patients to us. This is a more effective and ethical way to market ourselves, attracting more patients and increasing revenue.

Radical Honesty: Why Truth Wins Every Time

Honesty is the best policy is not just a statement but a fact. It makes our lives much easier and even profitable. It is common knowledge that speaking the truth is often easier than living a lie.

When we speak the truth, we don't have to remember what we said; we can be more confident, and our body language is much more assertive and trustworthy.

When we lie, our body language often gives us away. We feel uncomfortable, experience a sense of guilt, and most importantly, we must remember the lie we told earlier so that we can maintain it. We are always scared of getting caught.

So, despite knowing that Honesty is the best policy, why do we still lie?

Let's see the reasons for us to lie and the negative consequences of lying when it comes to Medical practice:

- We are afraid of speaking the truth because **we believe that if we tell the patient the complete truth, for example, about the prognosis of the surgery or the poor expected results of the treatment, they might run away and not undergo the operation or treatment with us.** This belief stems from our tendency to treat patients as if they are unwise and stupid. If we spend enough time with the patient, educate them, and demonstrate our sincere intent, most patients will be more than willing to continue with us. Suppose any patient is not willing to accept the truth and is seeking a miraculous cure. In that case, it may be better not to undertake the surgery for this patient.
- **We lie because we are scared to tell the patient or family of the complications of the treatment or surgery that has happened in our hands.** We have covered this topic elsewhere in the book on how to convert these potential crises into opportunities by being truthful and compassionate in handholding.
- **We lie because we feel insecure that the patient may go to our 'competition'** and get their treatment done there. This point is also covered elsewhere in this book.

- **We lie because we are scared of the medico-legal implications.** What we have again discussed is that having a complication is not a crime, but lying about it is a crime, so lying is detrimental here as well.

Our purpose in treating any patient is to help them. However, another important purpose of our interaction with the patients is to establish trust with them and their families and then have them become our brand ambassadors, referring more patients to us. If our lies are caught, which they would be in a matter of time, we are surely going to lose all the trust that we have built with them, and this patient would never come back to us and would never refer any patients. They may even become the opposite of our brand ambassador and actively discourage others from coming to us.

We all hate being lied to. But when it comes to health, we are even more scared of trusting someone with our body if we doubt their honesty.

Pushing Patients Towards More Expensive Options is Inviting Trouble

When a patient is being counselled for surgery, often the surgeon or the surgical counsellor tries to encourage the patient to opt for the more 'premium' package with a better lens, implant, cardiac stent, etc.

Some centres even 'incentivise' the surgical counsellors to book more 'premium' and more profitable packages.

This 'desperation' to convince the patient and family to opt for more expensive packages is evident to the patient and erodes their trust in the surgeon.

They are more likely to view the whole hospital as money-minded, are more likely to bargain and complain about the expenses, **and their expectations from the surgery become unrealistic because, often, while 'selling' these expensive options, the counsellors promise them the benefits in an exaggerated manner.**

When a patient has such high expectations from the surgical results, they are likely to be disappointed and are more likely to complain about the less-than-miraculous results. These patients had already formed an opinion earlier that the hospital is more money-minded. When they don't get the expected miraculous results, they feel cheated. They are likely to badmouth the hospital and the surgeon.

So, selling the more expensive package sometimes massively backfires.

Educate: Don't Manipulate

What I prefer to do and advise my friends to do is not to push the more expensive and premium options. One must understand that if a patient can afford it, they will likely opt for the best available option. But if they select that better option by their own choice, rather than being pushed, they are likely to be more satisfied.

Before discussing various options with the patient, the surgeon or counsellor must first listen to the patient and their family.

Try to gauge what is more important for them:

- Are they cost-conscious?
- Are they more concerned about insurance coverage?
- Are they quality-conscious and want the best for the patient?
- Are they more concerned about discomfort?

Once we have assessed the patient's and the decision maker's fears and objections, we must counsel them accordingly. We must reassure him and answer all the asked and unasked objections to make him comfortable.

Tell them about the various options available, right from basic to the most premium ones. Tell them honestly what benefits they will get when they go for the premium option. At the same time, **reassure them that the basic choice is also decently good (or else we would not be even offering it to our patients).**

Tell them the incremental benefit is small, and there would not be a wonder cure if they go for the premium package. **This is important to cap expectations in case the patient chooses the premium package.** Now, let them choose which option they want and answer their questions honestly. Towards the end, guide them gently towards the right choice.

In my almost three decades of practice, I have observed that patients typically opt for the best possible option if they can afford it, even if the incremental benefit is small.

They realise that it is a one-time decision, and no one likes to cut corners when it comes to their health, except when they genuinely cannot afford it. Since the choice is their own, without being pushed, and we have not promised the patient the moon, they accept the post-op results more happily, rather than expecting miraculous results. The patient also appreciates that we, unlike others, are not pushing for more expensive options and thus develops more trust in us and our systems.

For patients who cannot afford the more expensive premium options, we inform them that the basic choice is also nearly as good. As a result, they don't feel that they are receiving inferior quality treatment and are thus more likely to feel satisfied.

Branding With Integrity: Let the World (and Yourself) Know Our Values

Every individual has certain values that drive them. Similarly, every organisation, whether it has a staff strength of 2 or 2000, also has its values. It is essential to identify the values that drive us and document them in a place for our reference and clarity.

Values have an inward-looking and outward-facing role. The inward-looking role is what drives us and our organisation to do what we are doing. The common shared values within the organisation help to keep everyone in the team on the same page and share a common drive to achieve the organisation's goal.

The outward-facing value is the opinion that our customers and associates have about us. This includes our patients, their families, our colleagues, suppliers, staff, referring doctors, consultants, and others. The first thought that comes to their mind when they think of our organisation is our value system.

This also relates to the trust they have in our organisation and whether they are willing to deal with us.

For example, when we rebranded our practice to Synergy Eye Care, considerable thought was put into defining our name and values. I love to educate and empower my patients, and I want them to be partners in their eye care. Hence, we chose the name 'Synergy'.

Then, we selected the four values that we felt were most important for our practice: **Competence, Integrity, Safety, and Compassion.** We incorporated these four values into our brand logo, ensuring they are reflected in all our internal and external communications.

Competence is important to us, as we want every member of our organisation to do their best in whatever they do. It may be the surgeon performing the surgery or the housekeeping staff member doing the cleaning. We all strive to do our job in the best possible manner. Therefore, if I come across a procedure that I can perform but am not the best at, I do not hesitate to refer it to a colleague who can do a better job than I can.

Integrity is essential to win the trust of patients who surrender their precious eyes to our care. Integrity in our dealings with fellow doctors, vendors, and others is also a crucial component of our ecosystem. This has paid us rich dividends, with excellent trust among our patients and fellow doctors. In our model, where visiting consultants utilise our facilities, it is this trust in us that has given them the confidence to come to us, recommend us to their doctor friends, and thus contribute to our growth.

Safety is important when dealing with the human body, especially when it comes to something as delicate as the eyes. The culture of avoiding mistakes and reporting them as soon as possible, if errors do occur, is instilled in every team member. This has enabled us to get NABH certification at our centres, and we often exceed the safety norms required by NABH.

Compassion remains essential when interacting with individuals who come to us with their suffering. Making them comfortable relieves half their problems. This compassionate attitude must start with the guard or valet parking person, all the way up to the surgeon or Doctor in charge.

The advantage of announcing the Values that drive our brand is that—

- It informs the patients and their families what to expect when they visit us.
- It also serves as a constant reminder for every member of our team, ensuring we remember the promises we make to our patients and stay motivated to maintain our standards.
- It also helps to align a new staff member, a doctor, or a new referring doctor or visiting Doctor with what is expected of them when they work with us.

As with everything else, these Values should not be just words but should come with honest and genuine feelings, 'Dil Se'.

Key Takeaways

1. Being ethical is more profitable.
2. Trust is the most valuable asset we can have from our patients.
3. Winning a patient's trust will open the doors to success.
4. Honesty is still the best policy.
5. Suggest and help patients make informed decisions; don't push them towards more expensive options.
6. Know, document, and display the values of our organisation.

Chapter 9

The Synergy Model: Make Patients Partners in Their Healthcare

Establishing Synergy: A Two-Way Street

After examining a patient who had been coming to me for a long time, I advised him to have cataract surgery. As usual, after briefly explaining the disease and the proposed surgery to him, **I asked if he had any questions or would like to know about something else.**

He said he trusted me completely and, hence, did not feel the need to ask any questions. I responded by saying that it is perfectly okay to ask questions. Asking questions doesn't mean that he doesn't trust me. I appreciate patients who are eager to be more informed about their disease and its treatment.

Even though they trust me to do what is best for them, I would still like them to understand the process.

If patients understand the disease and the rationale behind the treatment and post-operative precautions, they are more likely to follow the post-operative instructions, take better care of their eyes, and have

more realistic expectations of the treatment.

I told him that this treatment is a partnership between us, and we both have to work together to achieve a better result.

This would be possible only when he understands what we are doing and why we are doing this.

I appreciate patients who research their health online and then return to me to ask questions and seek clarification. It is better to spend time explaining the disease before the surgery than to do it afterwards.

The patient understood the concept and was impressed by our openness to answering his questions; he was also satisfied with the outcome after the surgery.

When interacting with a patient during a consultation, it is a good idea to involve them in the decision-making process. A one-sided information where the Doctor tells the patients what to do doesn't work very well.

Moreover, nowadays, most patients will anyway 'Google' their diseases and will come up with some genuine and some non-genuine information.

We should educate them and provide them with proper, more scientific advice to satisfy their need for information so that they can better align with us.

We must understand that, more often than not, patients are unable to grasp all that has been told or explained to them. It happens because they are in such awe that they can grasp only a part of what is presented to them, and often, what they grasp selectively may not be the actual fact.

One can do this exercise at our next consultation. After our usual explanation about the disease or treatment, ask the patient or family to repeat what they have understood. We would be surprised to find that they understand and grasp only a limited number of things.

Patients and their families need to understand the disease and treatment options thoroughly to ensure they make informed decisions, are involved in the decision-making process, and know what to expect from the treatment.

This is especially useful in cases of complex surgeries with a relatively poorer prognosis. The patient must be aware of the expected benefits and should not expect miracles.

An aware and involved patient or family is more likely to maintain better follow-up and continuation of treatment, especially for diseases that require repeated and regular visits, such as Diabetic Retinopathy, Retinal diseases, Glaucoma, and corneal conditions. If the patient doesn't understand the importance of these regular follow-ups, they are likely to become irregular, thereby increasing the risk of complications.

One of the most significant advantages of involving patients and their families in understanding the disease and planning treatment is that they don't have unrealistic expectations of us and don't blame us in cases where the results are less than satisfactory, or even in cases of complications. They appreciate our efforts, not just the results.

This patient education helps us improve our treatment outcomes, which is beneficial for our practice.

It also means more regular patient visits. Dealing with these well-educated and informed patients becomes more pleasurable and enjoyable. The majority of patients appreciate being empowered to make decisions, which helps in the journey of converting patients into fans who will refer more patients.

Key Takeaways

1. Educate the patients and attendants.
2. Keep them involved in decision-making.
3. Answer their queries honestly and transparently.
4. Better to spend time with the patient answering questions before the surgery than giving explanations (which sound like excuses) after the surgery.
5. Educate the patients to spread our message to the general public.

A Quick Ready-Reference Summary and Recap

Here's a concise and scannable recap of the key points covered in the book, designed to help us scale up and thrive ethically in our medical practice.

1. **Let Patients Chase Us – Don't Sell, Educate**

   Avoid appearing desperate, even if it is driven by concern. Educate patients thoroughly, offer them options, and let them make informed decisions. This builds trust and makes them want to return rather than feel pushed.

2. **Focus and Refer – Specialisation Builds Credibility**

   Admit our limits. Patients respect doctors who are honest about their expertise and refer to other specialists when needed. It elevates us as a trusted authority in our domain. To be an expert in our field, it is necessary to admit that we may not be so in other fields.

3. **Be Human, Not God – Promise Effort, Not Results**

   Reject the "God complex." Patients calling us "God" is a red flag. Emphasise our effort and expertise, but be honest about uncertainties. This sets realistic expectations and avoids disappointment. Guarantee them our best efforts, not miraculous results.

4. **Own Our Complications – Transparency Over Denial**

Surgical complications happen. Don't deny them. Acknowledge, explain, and reassure. Patients value our courage to face problems head-on, and this builds lifelong trust.

5. **Run Toward the Patient After a Complication**

   Don't disappear when things go wrong. Personally follow up, answer questions, and offer support. Proactive communication in challenging moments often converts frustration into gratitude.

6. **Turn Problems into Opportunities**

   A complication, if managed with honesty and empathy, can make a patient our biggest fan. These moments test our ethics, and when we pass, patients become our advocates.

7. **Praise Our Peers – Ethical Collaboration Wins**

   Avoid badmouthing other doctors. It weakens our credibility and the profession's image. Instead, praise good work, even from competitors. This builds goodwill and trust with both patients and colleagues. This will also build us a genuine referral chain.

8. **Welcome and Act on Negative Feedback**

   Don't get defensive. Feedback reveals blind spots and shows patients that we care about improvement. Thank those who complain — they're helping us grow.

9. **Connect with the Child – Earn the Family's Loyalty**

   When treating children, speak directly to them, make them feel comfortable, and show empathy. A happy child earns us the trust of parents — and likely, the whole extended family.

10. Ethical Practice is Profitable

Doing the right thing is not just moral — it's smart business. Patients can sense sincerity, and ethical behaviour creates powerful word-of-mouth referrals.

11. Radical Honesty Builds Unshakeable Trust

Lying to patients might save face in the short term, but it always backfires. Truth earns trust. If we make honesty our policy, our practice becomes stronger and more resilient.

12. Don't Push Expensive Options – Respect the Patient's Choice

Present all options transparently. Let patients choose based on their needs and budget. Avoid hard-selling "premium" treatments — patients trust us more when we guide, not sell.

13. Declare Our Values – Let the World Know What We Stand For

Identify and share our practice's core values. Patients and team members align more easily with a doctor or organisation that has a clear moral compass and purpose.

14. Create Synergy – Treat Patients as Partners in Care

Empower your patients through education and collaboration. When individuals are engaged in their own treatment decisions, they're more likely to be loyal, satisfied, and compliant.

A Bonus

Start Your Practice Immediately With a BANG with ZERO Investment

The previous practical tips shared are guaranteed to be helpful to us when dealing with patients, whether in a job or running an independent practice.

However, starting and maintaining our practice, especially an Ophthalmology practice, is becoming more challenging nowadays, even more so when we are in a metro city like Delhi.

Patients prefer to visit an eye centre that is fully equipped with all the modern gadgets and types of equipment and is conveniently located. They also like to visit a place where all the facilities are available under the same roof, rather than wasting their time visiting different centres.

Some of the challenges in starting or even maintaining an ophthalmology practice are:

- Real estate cost of purchase or rent
- Cost of Interiors
- Cost of staffing, electricity, and other expenses.
- Registration and other legal compliances

- Empanelment with Insurance, TPA, and Government Panels
- A Good Cashless team to handle the cashless cases and recover the payments from Insurance companies and Panels
- NABH accreditation and various other compliances, including fire safety, HOTA for corneal transplant, pharmacy license, etc.
- OT licenses and records
- Ophthalmic and OT equipment purchase and maintenance which is very expensive, especially in Ophthalmology. The cost of Maintenance (AMC, CMC) is also prohibitive. The life of the equipment is also short and requires regular upgrades with technology, making it more challenging to achieve a return on investment (ROI) on these.
- Getting the right kind of technical employees like Nurses, OT assistants, Optometrists, Assistant Doctors, Anaesthetists, etc.
- Maintaining the HR department
- Availability of all the Sub-specialists of ophthalmology under one roof for cross referrals so that the patient need not get inconvenienced
- Accounting and legal compliance
- Medical Records Section
- CSSD and OT sterilisation department
- Marketing and Printing work
- Etc, etc.

These challenges are faced not only by newcomers but also by established practitioners with established centres nowadays due to increasing legal compliance and the rapid change of technology, which is expensive for a single practitioner to keep up with.

These high costs sometimes lead to desperation among us and **prompt us to push patients for surgeries or higher packages. This pushes patients away from us**, creating a vicious cycle that leads to dissatisfaction within the practice.

Working without the pressure of immediate earnings to pay EMIs is not only more peaceful, but it will also lead to faster growth and happier, more trusting patients.

- How can we achieve this in today's world, when patients expect to find every facility when they visit us?
- How do we achieve this without burning a hole in our pockets, whether we have the funds or not, and without the pressure of EMIs on a loan that we may need to take?

These difficulties often draw newcomers towards jobs with limited growth opportunities and limited independence.

Established practitioners who don't have the next generation coming into their practice often lose interest in expanding or even maintaining their practice. As a result, their practice slowly decays due to a lack of keeping the equipment up to date and maintaining all Necessary Insurance, Panels, and Accreditations.

Is There a Solution to This Ever-growing Problem?

- Of course, there is a win-win solution in the form of group practice where we share the resources.
- Solo practice is on its way out, and group practice is already here to stay.

There are two options for Group Practice.

- One option is to find a like-minded person or persons, pool your resources, and build it from scratch. It still requires a significant investment and considerable effort to establish a place, equip it well, obtain all the necessary licenses, staff it properly, implement the required systems, and conduct effective marketing.
- The other option is to join an established Group Practice Model which gives us all the independence, a good team of doctors to work with and refer our patients to, a well-equipped centre with up-to-date machines which are upgraded and maintained regularly, all the legal compliances and licenses, all the cashless facilities of Insurance and Panels, well-established accounts section, team of paramedics, etc.

The advantages of joining a centre as a visiting consultant on a revenue-sharing model like this are that there is **no investment required, and the practice can start with all the necessary facilities from day one.**

When one joins this kind of practice, these are the essential considerations that have to be kept in mind:

- There should be no 'poaching' of our patients there, and the centre should have a clean record of having enough doctors on board who can certify that this centre does not try to steal away their patients.
- The visiting consultants should get proper respect in the centre so that they feel as if it is their centre. Their patients should get the same level of care as those of any other consultants in the centre.
- The accounting system and records should be completely transparent, and the revenue-sharing system should be straightforward, easy to understand, and implement to prevent any misunderstandings in the future.
- There should be a decent record of satisfied visiting consultants in the system.
- The team of doctors at the centre should be well-qualified, covering all sub-specialities of ophthalmology so that patients can access all services under one roof.
- In the event of any surgical complication, the centre should have a well-defined protocol and system in place to manage both medical and legal challenges.
- The ethical and moral values of the centre should align well with our values.
- In addition to the above most essential points, other obvious factors, such as location, quality of construction, quality of facilities, and equipment, will also play a role in the decision.

You may wonder:

Does a setup like this exist?

Yes — it does.

At Synergy Eye Care, Delhi NCR, we've successfully run this collaborative group practice model for the past 9 years. Over 25 independent ophthalmologists currently operate from our centres — all without upfront investment, overhead stress, or compromise on ethics.

This model gives you:

- Complete independence in managing your patients
- Access to a state-of-the-art facility with top-tier equipment
- A supportive team of sub-specialists for internal referrals
- Established legal, administrative, and insurance frameworks
- Transparent revenue-sharing without hidden terms
- Ethical alignment — no patient poaching, no pressure-selling

Whether you're just starting or an experienced practitioner seeking sustainable, low-pressure growth, this system is designed to help you thrive ethically, efficiently, and immediately.

Want to Learn More? Let's Continue this Conversation

If this book resonated with you — if it shifted how you see your practice, your patients, or your purpose — I'd love to hear from you. Share your reflections, experiences, or small changes you've made. Whether you're just starting or a seasoned practitioner, your story matters and can inspire others.

- Connect with me on LinkedIn: **www.linkedin.com/in/drvinaygarodia**

If this book helped you, please share it with a colleague, student, or friend who might benefit from a more human, trust-based approach to medicine.

To explore these ideas further, whether through a one-on-one call or a chat about group practice, scan the QR code below to message me on WhatsApp (+91-6262-339-333). A pre-filled message will help us start the conversation.

Let's keep the dialogue going and bring more empathy, trust, and humanity back into medicine.

With gratitude,

Dr. Vinay Garodia